30 Days of

Hope

in an Unstable World

A DEVOTIONAL JOURNAL
on the Book of Jeremiah

MELISSA SPOELSTRA

30 Days of Hope in an Unstable World
A Devotional Journal on the Book of Jeremiah

CONTENTS

INTRODUCTION

Life can be rough sometimes. Relationship struggles, health challenges, financial strain, and everyday demands can make life seem overwhelming. In those times, we're often tempted to respond with worry, fear, doubt, or bitterness. But God offers us a better choice. He calls us to surrender our wills to His and place all our hope in Him.

This was the message of the prophet Jeremiah to the people of Judah—a message that is relevant to us, too. In this devotional, we will briefly explore six themes from Jeremiah's writings that call us to put our hope in God alone. His words encourage us that, because of our merciful and trustworthy God, hope-filled living is possible even in an unstable world.

Keep in mind that the Book of Jeremiah is not arranged chronologically, so it may feel a little disjointed. That's why this devotional is arranged by theme, not by chapter of the Old Testament book that bears the prophet's name.

Whether you're facing everyday challenges or a major crisis, you'll be encouraged by Jeremiah's message (which I explore in depth in my Bible study, *Jeremiah: Daring to Hope in an Unstable World*). This man of God found himself in very tough personal circumstances, yet he was able to keep his heart soft and hopeful through it all, trusting in the faithfulness of his God.

Each of the six chapters has a brief introductory section followed by five days of reading, scripture, prayers, and journaling. For those who enjoy it, each chapter also includes a simple coloring page around the theme of hope as well as two notes pages for you to add any additional thoughts and ideas that come to mind as you do your daily devotional times.

To stay on pace to complete the book in thirty days, you'll need to incorporate each chapter's introductory material into your first day's reading. However, feel free to move at your own pace. You may want to read the introductory material on one day and the remaining five days over the rest of the week. It's always fine to go at the pace that works best for your life.

Now, join me as we discover God's promises of hope for our life and circumstances. Let's dare to hope together!

Raising the White Flag

Surrender

1

When I discovered your words,
I devoured them.
They are my joy and my
heart's delight,
for I bear your name,
O LORD God of Heaven's Armies.

Jeremiah 15:16

Have you ever felt like you were right on the brink? Just one more emotional strain, relational conflict, financial setback, or physical ailment would send you right over the edge, causing you to want to give in and quit. The prophet Jeremiah gives us a glimpse into the instability in his own life. He encountered family and ministry problems and even got into some legal trouble. It's easier to relate to a guy who certainly never pretended to have it all together.

In the midst of Jeremiah's personal troubles and those of the surrounding culture, God gave him a message of surrender. But this call to surrender wasn't permission to drop out and throw in the towel because of life's many hardships. Though it can be tempting to consider giving up as a parent, employee, or friend when the going gets tough, God calls us to a different kind of surrender. Through the prophet Jeremiah, God called the people of Judah to trust in Him by surrendering to His leading instead of trying to sort out life from their limited vantage point. And God gave Jeremiah plenty of opportunity to demonstrate how to do this. Again and again, we see him looking to God's ways—made known through God's Word—over his own perspective. Jeremiah said,

> When I discovered your words, I devoured them.
>> They are my joy and my heart's delight,
> for I bear your name,
>> O Lord God of Heaven's Armies.
>>>> Jeremiah 15:16

We can learn a lot from this humble prophet's example. See if the overarching theme of surrender in Jeremiah's life and writings echoes into your own white flag anxieties.

Hope

DAY 1
No Excuses

"O Sovereign LORD," I said, "I can't speak for you! I'm too young!"

The LORD replied, "Don't say, 'I'm too young,' for you must go wherever I send you and say whatever I tell you."

Jeremiah 1:6-7

Jeremiah was the son of a priest living in a small town in the land of Benjamin, the least significant of the twelve tribes of Israel. He emerged during a time of great political upheaval as Babylon, Egypt, and Assyria rivaled for world domination. Against this unrest, God called Jeremiah to deliver His message.

Jeremiah first responded to God's call with many reasons why he couldn't do what God asked of him. Choosing to obey God would cost him family relationships and social standing. He also told God he was too young (Jeremiah 1:6-7).

Jeremiah made excuses, but God met every one of them with an assurance of His divine help and power. Eventually Jeremiah chose to believe and obey God despite his doubts and fears. In faith he followed God instead of giving in to his insecurities.

What nudging from God's Spirit have you been hearing lately? What plan has He revealed that will entail giving up some things you'd rather not? What excuses have you been making to get out of following God's clear leading? Jeremiah found that, although following God wasn't always easy, surrendering to God brought blessing while making excuses resulted in suffering consequences. As you consider what is holding you back from complete surrender to God, listen for God's voice of help and power assuring that He will empower you in every situation.

Prayer

Sovereign Lord, thank You for giving me a glimpse into Jeremiah's life to see that You call ordinary people like me who struggle with surrender, too. Thank You for being patient with my questions and reservations as I seek to discern your calling on my life. I pray that You will allow me to see that Your power is greater than any obstacles I face (or think I will face) and Your faithfulness is stronger than my weaknesses. Give me the courage to surrender myself to You. In Jesus's name I pray, amen.

How has the Holy Spirit been speaking to you lately?

What sacrifice(s) might God be asking you to make in your life?

What excuses have you made to avoid obeying God's promptings?

When you obeyed God in the past, what was the result? How might your past experiences give you assurance today?

DAY 2

Surrender
and
Popularity

So the officials took Jeremiah from his cell and lowered him by ropes into an empty cistern in the prison yard. It belonged to Malkijah, a member of the royal family. There was no water in the cistern, but there was a thick layer of mud at the bottom, and Jeremiah sank down into it.

Jeremiah 38:6

Jeremiah's message to the people was very unpopular because he foretold the destruction of the nation by the hands of the Babylonians. Yet Jeremiah faithfully proclaimed God's words over and over, and he began to get a reputation as a prophet of doom and gloom. No wonder Jeremiah wasn't too keen on being obedient. He knew he wouldn't gain any friends.

I know we like to pretend popularity was something we outgrew after high school, but many of us are still trying to find the right lunch table decades later. How many of us have felt left out after scrolling through our friends' social media posts? People-pleasing can influence our words, actions, and attitudes. We want people to like us. What about those times when totally yielding to God might upset our spouse, friends, or family members? God calls us to be faithful and obedient even when we must stand alone.

When Jeremiah boldly proclaimed God's message of surrender to the Babylonians, he faced opposition from government leaders. In an effort to silence him, King Zedekiah ordered that he be placed in a large cistern. Jeremiah discovered that obedience doesn't always mean that life will be easy. In Jeremiah 38:6, he found himself at the bottom of a pit, realizing that God values character and obedience over personal comfort or human applause.

How about you? How could completely yielding to the Lord in your life possibly affect those around you? Would they talk about you behind your back or think you've become a fanatic? What audience most greatly influences your daily decisions? Even though surrender won't always bring you popularity, God says He will bless you. His good plans might not always feel good in the moment, but obedience affords great long-term benefits. God promised to take care of Jeremiah and longs to shower us with His comfort as well.

Prayer

For today's prayer, follow the prompts below:

Almighty God, forgive me for worrying about what people might

think if I _____

(a step of obedience God wants you to take).

If I follow Your leadership, I am afraid _____

_____ (what you fear others might think or do).

Give me the courage of Jeremiah to do what You ask, even if it might

cost me _____

(what you think you may be sacrificing).

God, I know that I can trust You with the outcome.

In Jesus's name I pray, amen.

Have you ever chosen to do what was popular instead of what was right? What was the outcome? What did you learn?

Who is someone you admire for risking popularity or approval to obey God?

Think of a time when you obeyed God even though it affected your relationship(s) with others. How did God bless your surrendering to Him?

Why do you think surrendering to God is so unpopular in today's culture?

DAY 3
Confirmation

But if I say I'll never mention the LORD
or speak in his name,
his word burns in my heart like a fire.
It's like a fire in my bones!
I am worn out trying to hold it in!
I can't do it!

Jeremiah 20:9

Once we lay aside excuses and determine to please God above people, what if we still don't know what God is saying to us? Did we really hear God say we should quit our job, set new boundaries with a family member, or start a new ministry? Jeremiah's messages from God seemed so clear, but he still sought confirmation. He stayed in close fellowship with God through honest dialogue coupled with deep study of His Word. While God can speak through anything or anyone, Jeremiah found God's confirmation most often through prayer, Scripture, and people. God also confirmed his word to Jeremiah by taking away his peace until he obeyed. In Jeremiah 20:9, Jeremiah described the unrest he felt until he obeyed God.

I also have had times when I have asked God to direct me by giving me peace about a decision. When we weren't sure about a medical decision after praying, seeking counsel, and searching God's Word, I asked God to take away the overwhelming peace I felt about the procedure if it wasn't His leading. I felt His peace and lightness about proceeding when usually I would be fearful about this type of procedure, and I never regretted the choice later.

By following Jeremiah's example of intimate dialogue with God and careful study of God's Word, we can begin to discern whether a thought or idea is from the Holy Spirit or just our own desire. We also can find affirmation through people, circumstances, and when God "burns" His word in our hearts as He did in Jeremiah.

Prayer

What is something you think God may be leading you to do or say but you are unsure? Note any Scriptures that might be relevant to what God's Word says about this decision. What do you sense the Holy Spirit telling you? Remember, His Spirit will never contradict His Word. Below, write a prayer, asking God to help you trust Him no matter what direction He leads you.

Think of a time when you sensed God's peace regarding a decision or a situation. Describe how you felt.

Think of a time when you did not sense God's peace regarding a situation or decision. Describe how you felt.

How can these past experiences help you in a decision you are facing right now?

DAY 4

Defining
Success

I hurt with the hurt of my people.

I mourn and am overcome with grief.

Jeremiah 8:21

I find this thinking creeping into my own soul at times: I follow God=everything should go well for me.

But this is not biblical. The list is long of those who followed God and faced hardship and difficulty as a direct result. People mocked Noah for his boat project. Joseph's brothers put him in a pit and sold him into slavery. David hid in caves on the run for his life from King Saul. Jeremiah preached boldly but no one listened. His family rejected him, and his government imprisoned him.

Jeremiah shows us that even the most faithful followers can feel anxiety and depression and struggle to believe God, especially when obedience led to rough circumstances.

Jeremiah didn't walk around pretending everything was great when it wasn't. He told God he was frustrated and confused. He asked God questions about justice, and then he listened to God's truth and comfort. He continued to trust as he worked through his complaints and doubts.

God invites us to come to Him and wrestle through our personal battles. These struggles don't mean we are unsuccessful Christians. Instead, they give us an opportunity to take our thoughts and emotions to God.

How do you define success in your life? Do you need compliant kids, a brilliant career, or a thriving ministry to feel a sense of worth and identity? According to Jeremiah's message, we find that true success is found in surrendering to God. Jeremiah learned that eternal things matter more than temporary ones. Jeremiah realized that blessing comes from making the Lord his hope and confidence. By making the Lord your hope and confidence, you too can experience the blessed life that leads to true success.

Prayer

What personal battle are you facing? Write out a prayer to God, expressing your thoughts, feelings, questions, and struggles that are weighing on your heart.

Why is the belief "I follow God=everything should go well for me" so popular in American culture?

Complete the following statement: For me, success is . . .

How might God be using your current circumstances to reshape your ideas about success?

What did Jesus teach about success? (Use your Bible if you need a little help.) Example: "But many who are first will be last, and the last first" (Mark 10:31, NIV).

DAY 5

White Flag
Anxiety

"They will fight you, but they will fail.
For I am with you, and I will take care
of you.
I, the LORD, have spoken!"

Jeremiah 1:19

Jeremiah faced one difficult situation after another. He struggled with depression. He was left in a cistern to die. He knew that according to God's message, the people of Israel were facing seventy years of captivity. Yet, during it all, he clung to the Lord. He trusted in God to take care of him.

At the same time, Jeremiah didn't try to sugarcoat his struggles. He called God's help uncertain and blamed Him for the suffering he endured. (Have you lashed out at God, too?) He held nothing back, and God responded to Jeremiah with comforting words, promising to take care of him.

Even though our circumstances may range from puzzling to downright depressing, we can know that God is the One who will take care of us, too. He doesn't leave us as orphans in a sea of questions, trials, and difficulties. He promises to walk with us. While we don't always get the answers to our questions, we always get His presence.

Jeremiah talked with God, devoured God's Word, and chose to stand alone—but confident of the Lord's presence and power. Read again Jeremiah 1:19 again.

Do you ever stuff your pain instead of honestly working through it with God? While raising the white flag isn't usually easy, its benefits are innumerable. Jesus surrendered to His Father's will, and it resulted in our salvation. He calls us to take up our cross and follow Him. When we yield our plans to His, He can use us to bring His message of hope to an unstable world so desperately in need of it.

Where is God calling you to surrender today? Is there something you've been holding back because of fear or uncertainty—a relationship, a material item, a habit? Lay it down right now and hear God's tender words saying "I will take care of you."

Prayer

Heavenly Father, thank You for being faithful and good, for keeping Your promise to never leave me or forsake me. No matter what I face, You are my Rock and my Salvation so I can entrust every part of my life to You.

Jesus, thank You for being obedient to the Father's will. Because You surrendered everything, I can experience forgiveness, grace, and hope today and for eternity. Thank You for showing me how to lead a surrendered life.

Holy Spirit, thank You for being the Comforter that the Father sends in difficult times like the ones I am facing. Please speak words of truth to me when I doubt God's goodness and sovereignty. Show me the path to take and I will go where You lead.

In Jesus's name I pray, amen.

What might it mean for you to "give up your own way, take up your cross, and follow me [Jesus]" (Matthew 16:24)?

In your opinion, why does surrender carry such negative connotations?

What benefits or blessings come when we surrender to God?

What might God be teaching you about surrender?

Notes

Notes

RECOGNIZING COUNTERFEITS AND THE REAL DEAL

Idolatry

2

Idols are worthless; they are ridiculous lies!
On the day of reckoning they will all be
destroyed.
But the God of Israel is no idol!
He is the Creator of everything that exists,
including Israel, his own special possession.
The LORD of Heaven's Armies is his name!

Jeremiah 10:15-16

Have you ever struggled with riding the roller coaster of circumstances? When people seem to like us, stress levels are low, and things are going well in our world, we soar. But then we spiral downward when people are critical, money gets tight, or unexpected situations throw us off the ride completely. While God created us to experience emotions throughout life's ups and downs, we must be careful about what we have given ultimate place or priority in our lives. If we aren't careful, we might find ourselves living in despair because we put our hope in things that don't ultimately satisfy.

Jeremiah wrote about the danger of putting anything above God in our lives.

Idols are worthless; they are ridiculous lies!
    On the day of reckoning they will all be destroyed.
But the God of Israel is no idol!
    He is the Creator of everything that exists,
including Israel, his own special possession.
    The LORD of Heaven's Armies is his name!
                    Jeremiah 10:15-16

Let's consider some of the ways that Jeremiah's prophecy helps us discern the difference between spiritual counterfeits and the real deal.

IN CHRIST
ALONE
my hope
IS FOUND

DAY 6
Forgetfulness

"Does a young woman forget her jewelry,
or a bride her wedding dress?
Yet for years on end
my people have forgotten me."

Jeremiah 2:32

As you read in Jeremiah 2:32, Jeremiah uses jewelry and wedding dresses as illustrations of things we rarely forget.

Even now I can remember the details of my dress, complete with lace and a long, satin train. I will never forget the large shoulder pads that were so popular back then. We remember things we value as important. Yet somehow in the craziness of our daily routines, schedules, meetings, and all the things we "must" do, God sometimes falls to the bottom of the list. We say He is our priority, but the focus of our time and attention might reveal that we sometimes settle for convenient counterfeits over true connection with God.

Through Jeremiah's words of prophecy, God asks us to remember Him and not allow anything or anyone to take His place in our lives. What do you never forget because you value it so greatly? In what ways do you struggle with forgetting God? As we elevate God in our lives and value Him above all else, we will find ourselves less prone to forget. We'll remember His love, His justice, and His desire to have a deep relationship with us.

Prayer

God of Great Compassion, I am sorry for giving myself to activities, distractions, people, and pursuits that cannot satisfy my soul. It's so easy to get caught up in what's right in front of me that I forget You. Change my heart, focus my attention, and remind me of what matters. Renew my desire and passion for You. May nothing else capture my attention but You. In Jesus's name I pray, amen.

How do you feel when your priorities are in their rightful place? How do you feel when they get mixed up?

When you look at how you spend your discretionary time, what takes priority?

What time-wasters do you want to eliminate from your daily routine, including any apps or other digital distractions?

What is a spiritual practice that once helped you connect with God but has now fallen by the wayside? What would it look like to reincorporate it?

DAY 7

Spotting
a Fake

"For my people have done two evil things:

They have abandoned me—

 the fountain of living water.

And they have dug for themselves cracked cisterns

 that can hold no water at all!"

Jeremiah 2:13

Through Jeremiah, God uses a word picture to illustrate the difference between idols and Himself. Jeremiah said that God is like a fountain of living water—fresh, pure, and unlimited in supply. Then he likened idols to cracked cisterns. Cisterns were holes dug into the ground or rock for storing rainwater. And cisterns with cracks were completely useless for holding even dirty, stagnant water.

When we seek after idols, it's like drinking from a cracked cistern. We put our trust in people, jobs, status, money, and any number of things that make us feel safe and loved. Idols can look satisfying and good (and may even quinch our thirst for a while), but they cannot deliver. Not in the long run.

Without divine direction and supernatural guidance, we can chase after idols that won't yield results. We need God's help to know where to invest our time, what opportunities to pursue, and how to make the best decisions.

When we go it alone—without drinking from the fountain of living water— we find ourselves exhausted, thirsty, and empty. Speaking through Jeremiah, God told how He felt about His people's cracked cisterns (2:13).

Trusting in God, obeying His Word, and walking closely with Him will quench our spiritual thirst. God offers us living water, but He never forces us to drink.

We need to evaluate which practices in our lives lead to drinking from the fountain of God and which lead us toward self-reliance and idolatry. While the rest of his culture built leaky cisterns, Jeremiah persevered in drinking from the fountain of God. As you lay aside your counterfeits and drink deeply from God's fountain, you'll find a quenching of your spiritual thirst that you'll want to share with others.

Prayer

Dear God,

Forgive me for creating an idol of _____.

I recognize that _____ cannot

give my life meaning or supply me with hope, which only You can

provide. Help me not to give _____

the attention or affection that only belongs to You. May my heart

remain restless until I find my rest, peace, and hope in You. Amen.

If Jeremiah were living today, what modern item might he use to illustrate the real deal (living water) versus the fake (faulty cisterns)?

What counterfeits have you tried to quench your spiritual thirst? What happened?

What idols tempt you most often?

How can you tell when an idol is taking hold in your mind and heart?

DAY 8
Counterfeit Consequences

"This is what the LORD of Heaven's Armies, the God of Israel, says:

'Even now, if you quit your evil ways, I will let you stay in your own land . . . But I will be merciful only if you stop your evil thoughts and deeds and start treating each other with justice; only if you stop exploiting foreigners, orphans, and widows; only if you stop your murdering; and only if you stop harming yourselves by worshiping idols. Then I will let you stay in this land that I gave to your ancestors to keep forever.'"

Jeremiah 7:3, 5-7

God is a good daddy. He loves His children too much to leave us settling for empty substitutes. In Jeremiah's day, God gave clear instructions through His Word and issued warnings through His prophet when the people got off track spiritually. He was willing to stop His plans for exile if His people would stop their idolatrous ways (Jeremiah 7:3, 5-7).

Eventually, after their continual disobedience, He followed through with the consequences He had warned them about—just as a loving parent would.

Sometimes in my life I look to people, retail therapy, food, or media consumption to quench my spiritual longing, and it feels good in the moment. However, when I live on a diet of soul junk food, the spiritual flab begins to affect my health. While the consequences may not present themselves immediately, the plaque slowly builds in the arteries of my relationship with God. Apathy, bitterness, or distance in my relationship with God can slip in unnoticed until a crisis or conflict uncovers their presence.

Settling for counterfeits brings consequences that affect our spiritual health and keep us from the good plans God has for us. As we keep our focus on God—the "real deal"—we can then more easily spot the fakes in our lives. God wants to give us Himself in the midst of a world that offers every kind of substitute.

Prayer

For today's prayer, ask God to show you the soul junk food that is detrimental to your spiritual health. Then write down what God says as a letter that God is writing to you.

Dear _____, (your name)

I love you,
God

In the past, how have you experienced the consequences of poor spiritual health?

How is worshiping anything but God harmful for you?
(See Isaiah 7:6.)

How is idol worship harmful on a cultural level?

How is God speaking to you about the idols in your life?

DAY 9

Resources

"But a beautiful cedar palace does not make a
great king!
    Your father, Josiah, also had plenty to eat
    and drink.
But he was just and right in all his dealings.
    That is why God blessed him.
He gave justice and help to the poor and needy,
    and everything went well for him.
Isn't that what it means to know me?"
    says the Lord.

Jeremiah 22:15-16

How we spend our money is a great indicator of what we value. When we put God first in our lives, we give generously to others rather than indulge our own wants and desires.

We often don't see ourselves as greedy. We certainly don't see ourselves as frauds! However, when we are consumed with a desire for more—a nicer house, a better vacation, even simple things like new carpet—we can allow greed to rule our hearts. And the outflow of that greed is a life that doesn't mirror the heart and actions of Jesus.

Aren't greed and the need for "more" what our world offers? It tells us through commercials, movies, and social media that things, people, and status will make us happy. It tells us that fame, romance, or some new product will ease the ache deep in our hearts. And when that idol doesn't deliver (and it never does), we lose hope and joy.

We do not have to be ruled by our greed. We can choose to lay aside our idols of consumption. And as we do, we will uncover resources that we can use to help others. When we examine our lives and spending habits, we'll find small sacrifices we can make to help those in need—in our own communities and around the world. We can be bearers of hope, and when we do, we gain a little hope ourselves.

Prayer

For today's prayer time, imagine Jesus sitting next to you. Picture what He looks like, what His gaze is toward you. In the quiet, ask Him to share how He feels about your relationship with stuff. Listen to His response. Remember, He is a gentle Shepherd and He does not use shame, but He does speak truth. Write down what you hear.

How has greed shown up in your life?

How can you recognize when culture is shaping your attitudes and actions regarding money and spending?

How do greed and the desire for "more" erode hope?

What might it look like for you to let go of the need for "more"?

DAY 10

Making a Fake

"Their gods are like

helpless scarecrows in a cucumber field!

They cannot speak,

and they need to be carried because they cannot walk.

Do not be afraid of such gods,

for they can neither harm you nor do you any good."

LORD, there is no one like you!

For you are great, and your name is full of power.

Jeremiah 10:5-6

Envision with me the women of Judah. They might have been drawing water from the well, preparing food in an outdoor kitchen shared by neighbors, or sitting around weaving cloth or sewing clothes. They reminisced about the stories of God from the past and surmised that their God must have lost His power because much bigger nations had become the playmakers with all the wealth, power, and control. So, logically, they determined that the gods of those nations must be stronger.

Instead of clinging to the God of their ancestors even when He seemed silent, the women of Judah decided to get themselves some new gods. They decided their religion was outdated and needed a modern makeover, so they incorporated some foreign gods and religious practices to make up for God's weakness. However, when it comes to the sovereign ruler of the universe, we must worship Him alone and dare to hope in Him even when He doesn't act when or how we'd like.

If we will take a good look in the spiritual mirror, we'll see that we are not that different from the women of Judah. We create our own version of God that isn't consistent with what His Word reveals. Sometimes our attitudes, actions, and lack of prayer reveal that we are making our own gods instead of trusting fully in God's ability to care for us. We fashion a god that doesn't intervene, a god who's involved only in the "big" things instead of the details, a god who is waiting for us to mess up. Those are counterfeit gods—not the true and living God.

The best way to get rid of these idols in our lives is to offer them up to God. And then we cling to who God is as revealed in Scripture, not as He seems in the moment. We hope in Him because He is a great God. When we study His Word, talk to Him, and deepen our relationship, we will see our idols for the counterfeits they are.

Prayer

Pray the following based on Jeremiah 10:12-16:

Lord God, You made the earth by Your power and preserve it by Your wisdom. In Your great knowledge You stretched out the heavens. You cause the clouds to rise over the earth. In your perfect timing, You send the lightning with the rain and release the wind from its storehouses. In contrast, I am foolish and I have no knowledge! I confess that my idols are false and my images and ideas about You are often inaccurate. My faulty perceptions about You are worthless; they are ridiculous lies! Destroy my limited perceptions of You, for You are far greater than I can comprehend. You are the Creator and Sustainer of everything that exists, including me. You are a good and caring God who deals perfectly with the events of my life, and The Lord of Heaven's Armies is Your name! Amen.

What false versions of God do you see in culture?

What false ideas of God have you believed as true (for example, the distant One, the disinterested God, the too-busy God)?

What experiences might have given you a negative, misshapen, or untruthful perception of God?

How has God shattered your false perceptions of Him?

Notes

Notes

OPENING OUR EARS

Listening

3

"Ask me and I will tell you remarkable secrets you do not know about things to come."

Jeremiah 33:3

It happened one night when I was with the gals at middle school youth group. They were sharing some communication issues they all seemed to be having with their parents. The resounding response went like this: "My parents don't listen. When I talk, I can see they are thinking about something else. They are busy, preoccupied, and my school or friend problems aren't important to them. Eventually, I just quit telling them all the details because they don't listen anyway, or they act like the things I'm concerned about are silly or unimportant."

This composite of multiple responses alarmed me. When I went home and sat down with my daughters to inquire about my own listening skills, I found they had similar feelings. I began to wonder: *if my listening skills are lacking with my own children who are physically present and asking for my attention, how much more do I struggle with listening to my Creator God?*

How about you? Are your spiritual ears open or closed? In studying Jeremiah, I see a resounding theme that occurs over and over. God wants His people to open their ears and listen to Him:

> "Ask me and I will tell you remarkable secrets you do not know about things to come."
>
> Jeremiah 33:3

Let's explore this theme in Jeremiah and some of the ways we can become better listeners in our relationship with God.

God gives
you a future
and a hope.

Jeremiah 29:11

DAY 11

Called
to Listen

Listen, you women, to the words of
the LORD;

open your ears to what he has to say.

Jeremiah 9:20a

As we read through Jeremiah's book, we can't help noticing the volume of references to listening. Time and time again, Jeremiah spoke about God longing for His people to listen to Him. On one occasion, Jeremiah even addresses the women specifically (see Jeremiah 9:20a).

The Hebrew word for listen is *shama*, and it means "to hear with attention or interest."[1] This isn't a casual kind of listening while looking at a phone or thinking through a grocery list. To have biblical "open ears" means to listen, respond, cooperate, maintain focus, and prove with your actions that you have heard what God is saying.

We, too, struggle with closed spiritual ears, don't we? Despite the gifts of God's living Word, His Spirit, His body of believers (the church), and the life of His beloved Son, we often find ourselves distracted and stubborn like the peers of Jeremiah. God is calling us to open our ears and be willing to hear.

---

1 Shama," http://www.biblestudytools.com/lexicons/hebrew/kjv/shama.html.

Prayer

Oftentimes, we don't hear God because we don't sit still or quiet long enough to hear Him speak. For today's prayer time, say, "Speak, LORD, your servant is listening" (1 Samuel 3:9). Then, sit in the silence and wait for Him to speak to you. If your mind wanders (which it will), gently bring your focus back on God by praying again, "Speak, Lord, your servant is listening." Try this spiritual practice for five minutes. In the space below, write down what you hear God say.

What distractions most often keep you from intently listening to God?

When are you more prone to listen to God? When are you more prone to ignore Him?

What has God done in the past to get your attention? What was the result?

Would those closest to you describe you as quick to listen, responsive, cooperative, focused, and living a life that reflects the faith you claim?

DAY 12

Reading with Curiosity

"O Sovereign LORD! You made the heavens and earth by your strong hand and powerful arm. Nothing is too hard for you!"

Jeremiah 32:17

Another way we listen to God is by reading His Word with curiosity. Do you remember the Curious George children's books? The man with the yellow hat often got frustrated with Curious George, but George's curiosity helped save the day on many occasions. We can learn from this little monkey to approach God's Word with an inquisitive posture. Rather than reading the Bible out of routine, obligation, or preparation for a lesson, what if we studied it with the intent of knowing God better? We could ask questions such as these:

- What can I learn about God—who He is, how He interacts with people, what the verses say about His character?
- What can I learn about myself—how I approach God, what He calls me to do/not do, how He expresses His love, what keeps me from experiencing Him more fully?
- What might God be saying about my current thoughts, attitudes, or actions?

As we seek to know God through His Word, we'll find He is the Potter and we are the clay (Jeremiah 18:6). We'll see Him as the Lord of Heaven's Armies (Jeremiah 51:5). We'll also find that Jeremiah knew Him as the Sovereign Lord for whom nothing is too difficult (32:17).

We can listen and know God better, too, as we study His Word with curiosity.

Prayer

For today's prayer time, read John 8:2-11 slowly with a curious eye. What questions come up for you? What is God showing you about Himself or yourself? Write a brief prayer based upon your thoughts about the reading.

What are some questions you have regarding verses, people, stories, or truths in Scripture? (For example, what did Mary and Joseph do with the gold the wise men gave Jesus?)

How might openness and curiosity create opportunity for a deeper relationship with Jesus?

What are the dangers of reading Scripture without a sense of curiosity?

As human beings created in the image of God, how does our curiosity reflect God's image?

DAY 13

Cling Like Underwear

"As a loincloth clings to a man's waist, so I created Judah and Israel to cling to me, says the LORD. They were to be my people, my pride, my glory—an honor to my name. But they would not listen to me."

Jeremiah 13:11

Another way we become better listeners is by clinging to God.

Do you like loose, baggy underwear? I don't either. Underwear doesn't look or feel good unless it fits snugly. Guys may choose between boxers and briefs, but we girls like our underwear to fit.

You might be wondering where this talk of underwear is going. Believe me, this Texas girl does not enjoy public conversations about private things. It doesn't take much to make me blush. However, God is the One who mentions the "unmentionables." He tells Jeremiah to go bury a new loincloth (underwear) in a hole. He then uses it as an illustration for how He created His people to be close to Him—to cling to Him (Jeremiah 13:11).

Unfortunately, the people of Judah refused to listen. I pray our response will be different. I hope we will be tight, personal, and intimate in our relationship with our God—clinging like underwear.

Prayer

For today's prayer, choose an everyday item nearby and write a prayer based on that item. For example, you might see a bird outside your window and write that You would hide under the shadow of His wings as you face a difficult situation.

What does clinging to God look like for you?

What people, situations, spiritual practices, Bible verses, or other things help you cling to God?

What hinders you from clinging to God?

Why does clinging to God help you hear Him more clearly?

DAY 14

Listen to
the Right
Voices

"Let these false prophets tell their dreams,
but let my true messengers faithfully
proclaim my every word.
There is a difference between straw
and grain!"

Jeremiah 23:28

Besides reading God's Word with curiosity and clinging closely to Him in a daily relationship, becoming a better listener requires that we listen to the right voices. Every day we are bombarded by a cacophony of messages. Between my mailbox, social media feeds, television shows, and daily interactions with others— even as I wait in the checkout line at the store—there is a constant barrage of information coming at me. There's no shortage of voices in the Christian realm either. It's great to talk, debate, and work through the issues related to trying to follow God. But how can we know that we are following the right leaders, listening to the right voices, and walking in God's truth in the many arenas of life? We don't want to be like the people of Judah in Jeremiah's day who didn't listen to God but rather chose to listen to other voices with a more popular message.

Jeremiah teaches us some principles of discernment:

- Consider the moral character of the messenger.
- Evaluate the message to see if it lines up with God's Word.
- Ask the right questions.

Jeremiah used a common food—grain—to explain that not every message nourishes our soul with truth. Some information is like grain, which was used for nourishment, but other information is more like straw, which was used for bedding. It might provide a temporary comfort, but it will still leave you with an empty spiritual stomach.

As we listen to God, we need His wisdom to know the difference between straw and grain. He will help us discern what will nourish our soul with truth and what will give us momentary comfort but leave us empty.

Prayer

Jesus, You alone are the Bread of Life. You are the nourishment my soul craves most because I was created by You and for You. Forgive me for settling for spiritual junk food that cannot satisfy. Forgive me for spending my time, thoughts, energy, and money on cheap counterfeits that will ultimately disappoint me and leave me empty. Create in me a deeper hunger for You, a hunger that drives me toward You as the source of my satisfaction. Nothing I desire compares to You. I love you. Amen.

How would you describe your spiritual diet?

What junk food do you consume that might feel good for a while but won't nourish your soul?

What is your favorite way to feed yourself spiritually? (podcasts, Bible reading, worship, silence and solitude, and so forth)

What spiritual nourishment might you need to feed on more regularly?

DAY 15

Keep Asking

Can any of the worthless foreign gods send us rain?

Does it fall from the sky by itself?
No, you are the one, O LORD our God!
Only you can do such things.
So we will wait for you to help us.

Jeremiah 14:22

Jeremiah modeled listening for us. We see that he approached God with confidence, rehearsing characteristics about who God is and how He behaves. He asked specific questions. He expressed his frustrations over things that didn't make sense to him. He admitted his own faults and asked God to correct him when he was wrong.

God welcomes our asking, too. Asking means dialogue. We don't have to stuff our doubts. Doubts are real, and everyone has them. What matters is what we do with them. Our doubt and confusion should lead us to think deeply, study, and ask questions.

I write down specific questions I have for God all the time. I put them in my Bible next to a passage I don't understand. I write them in my journal as I pray. I once asked God why the Book of Jeremiah seems like it isn't in order since it doesn't flow chronologically. Not five minutes later in my daily reading I found Ecclesiastes 7:13: "Accept the way God does things, for who can straighten what he has made crooked?" Yep. Got it, God—I don't need to straighten You out!

If God doesn't answer right away, keep asking. Take time to listen with the expectation that He will answer in His timing. In Jeremiah 14:22, Jeremiah wrote about the value of waiting on God:

We see the consistency of asking, listening, and knowing God in prayer all the way from Jeremiah through the entire span of the New Testament. This is a recurring theme. Ask, ask, and ask. Listen, listen, and listen some more!

God mostly answers my questions through His Word, but He sometimes uses other books, people, and circumstances. When God seems silent in my life, I usually discover that I've either stopped asking questions or stopped taking the time to listen for the answers.

What is keeping you from a close relationship with God in your prayer life? What is He saying to you today?

Prayer

For today's prayer, talk with God about a question or doubt you have been wrestling with. Be honest with Him about how you are feeling. When you have finished, spend a few moments in silence and listen for Him to respond. He may answer your question, or He may offer words of comfort, peace, or encouragement. Use the space below to write down what you hear Him saying.

How do you feel knowing that God can handle your questions?

What questions has God yet to answer for you?

What can be gained by waiting for God to answer your questions?

What questions might God have for you?

Notes

Notes

STAYING SPIRITUALLY SENSITIVE

Heart Issues

4

"The human heart is the most deceitful of
all things,
   and desperately wicked.
   Who really knows how bad it is?
But I, the LORD, search all hearts
   and examine secret motives.
I give all people their due rewards,
   according to what their actions deserve."

Jeremiah 17:9-10

Have you ever experienced spiritual chest pain? You ache inside over emotions you can't readily identify. All you know is that something hurts. Physically, hearts can experience any number of problems, such as leaky valves, aneurysms, or clogged arteries. Similarly, we have fragile hearts spiritually.

No matter what our heart issues are right now, we must be careful to allow God full access to our hearts. Glossing over issues, skipping to the next thing, and moving on in life without dealing with heart issues is much simpler than going through the softening process. Many of us have done this for years—especially in relationships with family and friends. We stuff our pain and continue living our lives without dealing with our heart issues. The great news is that allowing God to do the deep work fosters closeness with Him in the midst of our brokenness that is unbelievably powerful.

Jeremiah was no stranger to spiritual open-heart surgery. He endured rejection, betrayal, and taunting by his own people when he chose to follow God wholeheartedly. Yet he remained humble and teachable in his struggles. How did he do it? What can we learn from his message and example?

Hope

ANCHORS
THE *Soul*

HEBREWS 6:19

DAY 16

Heart
Evaluation

Search me, O God, and know my heart;
test me and know my anxious thoughts.
Point out anything in me that offends you,
and lead me along the path of
everlasting life.

Psalm 139:23-24

Heart issues can be complicated. At times we struggle to understand just what is going on inside of us. To uncover the deeper issues of our hearts, a helpful first step is asking questions: Lord, why do I feel so sad, distracted, or empty? We have to embrace the truth about our human heart defaults and give ourselves a regular heart evaluation. David understood this when he wrote Psalm 139:23-24.

I can be an expert heart evaluator—of other people's motives and heart attitudes, that is. If I don't check myself regularly, I find that I read into every word, expression, and body language cue to form a conclusion about how the other person feels and thinks, and I may be off course. With relationships, finances, and disagreements, we can all be too quick to see where others are wrong.

God is the One who searches all hearts and examines secret motives. Focusing on others' heart issues wastes time and distracts us from dealing with our own heart symptoms. But when we spend our mental and emotional energy allowing God to evaluate the sin in our hearts first, we usually find that we see others and their situations differently. By being aware of our personal tendencies toward sin and expending our time and energy on our own repentance, we can view others with more grace and less judgment. Psalm 139:23-24 should become our regular personal prayer. May we trust God to search our hearts, point out those areas that need tending and mending, and allow Him to lead us on a better path.

Prayer

Meditate on Psalm 139:23-24. Listen to God speak about those areas of your heart that need His intervention and healing, and then write them down in the heart graphic.

Why do we as human beings tend to avoid, ignore, or minimize the internal movements in our hearts?

What is your go-to strategy for handling difficult emotions in your heart?

What happens personally when you ignore your spiritual heart issues?

Recall a time when God performed spiritual heart surgery on you. How did God heal or change your heart?

DAY 17

Behavior Modification vs. Heart Change

"O Israel, my faithless people,
   come home to me again,
for I am merciful.
   I will not be angry with you forever.
Only acknowledge your guilt.
   Admit that you rebelled against the LORD your God
and committed adultery against him
   by worshiping idols under every green tree.
Confess that you refused to listen to my voice.
   I, the LORD, have spoken!"

Jeremiah 3:12-13

After taking some time to evaluate our hearts, our tendency is to go into "change my behavior mode." We say to ourselves, "Okay, now that I see the hardness, bitterness, and deception in my heart, I will get up every day and have my quiet time, go to church every Sunday (even when I'm tired), and try to watch less TV. That should help change my heart." However, when we over-concentrate on actions, we don't get to the root issues.

Trying to fix our hearts by trying to follow rules is not what God has in mind. Heart change happens internally first and then displays itself externally as we acknowledge and respond to the sin we've identified.

In Jeremiah 3:12-13, God instructed His people about heart change through the prophet Jeremiah. In these verses, Jeremiah presents three truths that lead to lasting change in life:

- *Know it.* Get honest with ourselves about how we feel and the sinful tendencies we harbor in our hearts.
- *Share it.* Bring your heart before a loving God who longs to offer us hope and healing.
- *Own it.* Accept personal responsibility for our mistakes—and accept the forgiveness God offers.

We can know, share, and own our sin because God in His mercy will forgive us and help us turn from it. He doesn't ask us to clean ourselves up, fix our bad behavior, and then approach Him. He welcomes us in our brokenness. He alone can change our hearts.

Prayer

During your meditation time today, contemplate the three truths from the previous page, and then write a prayer of confession to God.

- *Know it.* In what area (sinful habit, unhealthy relationship, and so forth) do you need to be honest with God?
- *Share it.* Be honest and transparent with God.
- *Own it.* How might you need to take responsibility?

Why do you think self-help resources (books, conferences, podcasts, and so forth) remain popular year after year?

Why is willpower alone ineffective in changing your heart?

Recall a time when you vowed to "do better" only to fall back into the same sin. How does Jeremiah 3:12-13 offer hope?

Picture giving your whole heart over to God. What emotions come up for you? Why?

DAY 18

Where Do Broken Hearts Go?

"My wayward children," says the LORD,
   "come back to me, and I will heal your
   wayward hearts."

"Yes, we're coming," the people reply,
   "for you are the LORD our God."

Jeremiah 3:22

Finding out I was having twins just ten days before I had them caused great fear in this gal who'd already experienced the birth of a singleton. I knew what to expect with a newborn. The thought of doubling that encounter freaked me out!

Sometimes our trials are not physical experiences, such as birthing a child, but they are emotional, mental, and spiritual labors. Such trials can birth great intimacy with Christ, but the process can be excruciating. Jeremiah knew this all too well as he is often referred to as the Weeping Prophet—rejected by his family and community, falsely accused and imprisoned, thrown into the bottom of a muddy pit, and found weeping over his people who refused to repent.

When we experience deep pain, we are vulnerable to bitterness, depression, and anxiety. God calls us to bring our broken hearts to Him.

In this world we will have trouble. We need to bring our troubles to the One who has overcome this world. That is our great God. God doesn't want us to ignore our problems, stuff our feelings, or pretend we aren't hurting. God wants us to come to Him, cling to Him, and trust Him even when we can't see Him and our lives seem to be falling apart. This is what it means to dare to hope in an unstable world.

Prayer

God of my heart, You know me inside and out. You know when I run from You and why I hide from You. Yet, You continually offer me your grace and mercy. You long for me to turn to You so You can heal me. Forgive me for trying to hide my heart from You. I lay my heart open before You and I trust You with what is inside. Take away my sin. Reveal to me any lies of the devil that keep me from You. Heal the pain from my past sin and hurts from other people. I cling to You as the Good Shepherd, my Loving Father, and the Redeemer of Broken Things. Amen.

What keeps you from bringing your whole heart before God?

What does the world offer to help you deal with a broken heart?

How might God use the broken places in your heart to bring about good in your life?

How can a healed heart bring glory to God?

DAY 19

Guard
Your Heart

Guard your heart above all else,

for it determines the course of your life.

Proverbs 4:23

Because our hearts are so sensitive, we must be careful to guard them.

In a world that offers easy and instant access to an overwhelming amount of information, guarding our hearts takes great intentionality. With remotes, keyboards, and screens increasing our exposure to harmful influences, we can easily become desensitized to the ways those influences can affect our hearts. God longs for us to keep our hearts soft. He asks us to guard what flows both in and out of them. Allowing the Holy Spirit and God's Word to be our "filter" helps keep our words and actions—and the actions and words of others—from damaging our hearts. Jeremiah said his people had lost their ability to blush. They became desensitized by the surrounding culture and failed to protect their hearts. He cautioned the people about how their thoughts and words might influence their hearts. He was challenging them to guard their hearts.

Prayer

Spend time in prayer, asking God what heart boundaries you might need to establish to provide protection for your heart. Write down what He says about the following areas:

Relationships:

Screen time:

Podcasts:

Books:

TV/Streaming:

Other:

John 10:10 says, "The thief's purpose is to steal and kill and destroy. My purpose is to give them a rich and satisfying life." How might this verse help you understand your heart?

Read Proverbs 4:23 again in several different translations. Jot down the words and phrases that stand out to you as significant or helpful.

How might guarding your heart be a way to love yourself as Jesus commanded in Mark 12:31?

How might guarding your heart be an act of worship before God?

DAY 20
With All
Your Heart

"If you look for me wholeheartedly, you will find me."

Jeremiah 29:13

God doesn't want half of our hearts. He wants our total devotion. Unfortunately, we often put more time and intentionality into planning our next vacation or birthday party than we do intensely pursuing God with our whole hearts. While offering God our leftovers, we wonder why we often seem to be losing the spiritual battle against sin in our lives.

God created us for fullness of life; and although sin has marred God's original design, He redeems us through Christ. God doesn't desire all of our hearts because He is possessive or controlling; He simply knows that we are designed for intimacy with Him. He knows that our halfhearted attempts at following Him will lead only to dissatisfaction, complacency, and mediocrity—leaving us wanting something more. When we don't find our satisfaction in God, we tend to look to empty substitutes that can never satisfy. So, God calls us to wholehearted devotion, and He leads us by His own example—offering His only Son to save us. He wants our wholehearted love in return. He promises that when we seek Him, we will find Him. And His hope never leads to disappointment!

Prayer

God Almighty, You deserve more than my half-hearted attempts at following You. I am sorry for chasing after things that don't ultimately satisfy. Like the prodigal son whose stomach longed for food from his father's house, I long for the food you provide my soul. Only You can meet the deepest needs of my heart, so I turn away from the things of this world and turn to You, the Lover of my soul. I put my heart and hope in Your loving and faithful hands. Amen.

How would you describe your devotion to God—halfhearted, wholehearted, or entirely differently?

Why do you think we as human beings are so prone to giving our hearts to other pursuits instead of chasing after God wholeheartedly?

Can you recall a time in your life when your halfhearted attempts at following Him led to dissatisfaction, complacency, and/or mediocrity? Describe what happened.

Can you recall a time in your life when you pursued God with all your heart, mind, soul, and strength? Describe that time in your life and the results of pursuing Him.

Notes

Notes

QUITTING THE BLAME GAME

Personal Responsibility

5

This is what the LORD says:
"Don't let the wise boast in their wisdom,
   or the powerful boast in their power,
   or the rich boast in their riches.
But those who wish to boast
   should boast in this alone:
that they truly know me and understand
that I am the LORD..."

Jeremiah 9:23-24

Who's your favorite "target"? When things go wrong in my world, I can find lots of places to assign blame. My husband, the church, my kids, or anyone nearby might find my finger pointed at them as responsible for my failure.

We come by this tendency quite honestly. Adam blamed Eve, and Eve accused the serpent at the scene of the very first sin. Ever since then, we have had to fight the urge to blame and have had to learn to take personal responsibility for our mistakes. God doesn't want us to grovel in shame but simply admit our shortcomings so that we can be forgiven and changed through His power.

The people of Judah wouldn't listen to Jeremiah's call to take personal responsibility. They continued to play the blame game. In Jeremiah 9:23-24, God called them to let go of their prideful attitude.

As we look to Jeremiah's Book, let's see if we can learn from their mistakes and take a posture of humility instead of pride.

MAY THE GOD OF HOPE FILL YOU WITH JOY & PEACE

ROMANS 15:13

DAY 21

Good
Discipline

"Is not Israel still my son,
   my darling child?" says the LORD.
"I often have to punish him,
   but I still love him.
That's why I long for him
   and surely will have mercy on him."

Jeremiah 31:20

Nothing can get under a parent's skin like a child who won't respond to appropriate discipline. One of my children says that another is to blame for his or her failure to complete a chore or make a wise choice. Then when I investigate and point out a child's sin or mistake, the blame can quickly turn to me. I'm told that I make unfair decisions, expect too much, or don't understand their lives. My discipline or consequences are viewed as measures to "ruin their lives." Over and over, I try to explain that if I didn't care, I wouldn't take the time and energy to correct, train, pray, and discipline.

While I try to parent as best as possible, I don't always get it right. However, God is the perfect parent. His kids (the people of Judah) often rebelled, but He continued to give them clear warnings and to follow through with consequences when they didn't respond.

God does the same with us. He isn't out to ruin our lives, but He uses whatever is necessary to get His children's attention when we are making terrible decisions. God is willing to watch us suffer the consequences of our poor choices if that's what it takes to bring us back into relationship with Him. However, He always does this out of His great love for us. Look for His Father's heart behind whatever correction He is giving and seek to be a teachable child.

Prayer

For today's prayer time, ask God to show you whether any difficulty you are currently experiencing is a result of poor choices you have made. Also ask Him to reveal His desires for you in this difficulty. Write down anything God says to you below.

How is proper discipline an act of love?

How might a parent's discipline be different from God's discipline?

How do you think God feels when He disciplines us?

Can you think of a time when God allowed you to experience the consequences of a poor choice so you would turn back to Him? Describe what happened.

DAY 22

Finding
a Target

"People from many nations will pass by the ruins of this city and say to one another, 'Why did the LORD destroy such a great city?' And the answer will be, 'Because they violated their covenant with the LORD their God by worshiping other gods.'"

Jeremiah 22:8-9

When I was a kid, my dad occasionally would wake everyone in the house and call us to hunt for his lost keys so he could get to work. The apple doesn't fall far from the tree—only with me it's my cell phone. I never remember where I left it and often blame my kids or husband for moving it. Usually, I find it in my purse or jacket pocket—right where I left it. Until it is found, I am sure that someone else is to blame. It's humbling when the facts prove that my accusations are unfounded.

The people of Judah had problems with blaming as well. They often claimed they were innocent of wrongdoing and denied that they worshiped idols. They did not want to take personal responsibility for playing a part in the consequences headed their way. Jeremiah gave them a warning in Jeremiah 22:8-9.

What are your targets for blame shifting when things go wrong in your world? What freedom could you find in admitting your faults instead of playing the blame game?

Prayer

Using Psalm 51:1-4 as a model, offer a prayer to God, taking responsibility for your actions and asking His forgiveness:

Have mercy on me, O God, because of your unfailing love. Please blot out the stain of my sins. I take responsibility for my actions and my rebellion. Against you, and you ultimately, have I sinned; I have done what is evil in your sight. Purify me from my sins, and I will be clean; wash me, and I will be whiter than snow. Create in me a clean heart, O God. Renew a loyal spirit within me. Restore to me the peace and joy that comes from trusting You and give me the desire and strength to obey You. Amen.

Who do you tend to blame for your mistakes?

How do you feel when you blame others for your faults and sinful actions?

How do you feel when you take responsibility for your actions?

How does taking responsibility for your sin impact your relationship with God?

DAY 23

Perilous
Pride

And if you still refuse to listen,
    I will weep alone because of your pride.
My eyes will overflow with tears,
    because the LORD's flock will be led
    away into exile.

Jeremiah 13:17

Admitting our faults requires letting go of pride. Pride is an elusive thing. It can take many forms. Simply put, it is an obsession with self. Apart from God's work in our lives, every one of us will make decisions to serve our own interests—to paint ourselves in the best light and work out situations to our benefit. This is the core of our sin problem. We all battle daily against the sin of pride.

Jeremiah pronounced judgments on the surrounding nations of Judah, and many of them were indicted for their pride.

God wept over the people of Judah's downfall of trusting in their wealth and skill. They deceived themselves into thinking that every good thing in their lives was their own doing. This attitude resembles the American mindsets of "I deserve it," "I am powerful," and "Look at all I have accomplished." Hard work, goal setting, and material goods are not inherently wrong, but we would be wise to remember that anything good we accomplish originated in God, who gave us the talent and resources.

Prayer

Use the following prompts to guide your prayer time:

Lord, forgive me for my prideful attitude regarding _____

_____.

I'm sorry for thinking I deserve _____.

Forgive me for trying to _____

instead of surrendering to You as Lord of my life.

I recognize that without You, I cannot _____

_____.

May I seek Your glory instead of my own, and may I seek You first in all I do. Amen.

Why does God oppose the proud (see James 4:6)?

Can you think of a time when your pride got you into trouble? What happened?

In what areas of your life do you see pride creep in most often and easily?

How can you cultivate a spirit of humility when you succeed or flourish?

DAY 24

Going through the Motions

"Don't be fooled into thinking that you will never suffer because the Temple is here. It's a lie! Do you really think you can steal, murder, commit adultery, lie, and burn incense to Baal and all those other new gods of yours, and then come here and stand before me in my Temple and chant, 'We are safe!'—only to go right back to all those evils again?"

Jeremiah 7:8-10

Pride also can affect our devotion to God. Though religious rituals can have great significance and can be holy acts through which we experience the presence and grace of God, we must be careful not to allow them to make us feel that we are somehow appeasing God or fulfilling some kind of duty or obligation. Religious rituals become empty when our motivation is anything other than our devoted love for God.

That's exactly what had happened to the people of Judah's worship: they were going through the motions. The priests were offering sacrifices, and false prophets were delivering messages they said were from the Lord, but their hearts were not right.

Can you think of seasons in your spiritual life when you have been going through the motions? I have found myself reading the Bible, serving in ministry, or even attending church out of duty or obligation, like checking off a box on a spiritual to-do list. While some spiritual disciplines require pushing through emotions of resistance, we must be careful not to allow our walk with God to become routine and empty.

Prayer

Lord, I come before You with an open heart, asking for Your help to see where I've been going through the motions in my relationship with You. Forgive me for the times I've allowed routine to replace genuine intimacy and I stopped seeking Your presence. Show me where I've become distant. Awaken my heart to Your love and give me a hunger to know You more deeply. Draw me into a greater love and passion for You. In Jesus's name, amen.

What spiritual practices (disciplines) have lost their meaningfulness to you in recent days? What spiritual practices are meaningful?

What would it be like for you to try new spiritual disciplines, such as solitude and silence, prayer journaling, or fasting from social media?

How can you guard against your spiritual practices becoming a check list or obligation?

How can you move from just "doing" things for God to truly "being" with Him?

DAY 25

Rescue with Repentance

This is what the LORD says:

"Stop at the crossroads and look around.

Ask for the old, godly way, and walk in it.

Travel its path, and you will find rest for your souls.

But you reply, 'No, that's not the road we want!'"

Jeremiah 6:16

Have you ever been driving the wrong way and your smart phone or GPS said, "Recalculating"? Then it rerouted you so that you turned back toward your destination rather than away from it. A similar concept happens in life when we get off course spiritually. Once we acknowledge we are moving in the wrong direction, we must turn around—repent—and go God's way, which leads us to the destination of intimacy with Him.

The people of Judah had a lot of experience in offering empty words. They cried out to God, declaring their intent to change their ways, but there was no repentance or reorientation of their lives, no turning away from sin and a simultaneous turning to God. Jeremiah spoke to the people about this in Jeremiah 6:16.

Instead of blaming others, ourselves, or Him, God calls us to turn from our sin and walk in trust and obedience. He is always faithful to redirect us as we take personal responsibility for our mistakes and ask for His help in navigating back onto His path for our lives.

Prayer

Below, write your own letter of repentance, your own declaration of turning away from your own path and turning back toward your Heavenly Father. He wants to lead you on the path of life and the road of intimacy with Him.

What or whom do you typically blame for sinful habits, attitudes, or behaviors?

Can you recall a time when you realized you were heading in the wrong direction? How did God get your attention?

Why might people resist or avoid the "godly way," even when they know it will bring peace, restoration, and hope?

How can returning to trust in God and obedience to Him lead to hope?

Notes

Notes

FINDING THE SOURCE
OF OUR HOPE

The Promised Messiah

6

"For I know the plans I have for you," says the LORD. "They are plans for good and not for disaster, to give you a future and a hope."

Jeremiah 29:11

We cannot escape this haunting feeling as we turn the pages of Jeremiah: the days of his prophecy sound uncannily like ours. While the symptoms may flesh out differently, the root problems of our modern culture profoundly parallel those of the nation of Judah. Like those people, we face a choice as individuals and as a nation to respond to God's call to hope. While despair seems to loom all around us, *we can find hope*. While our circumstances, conflicts, and problems may not improve, our hope is found in God's promised Messiah. Jeremiah said that He would come and save the people from their sin under a new covenant.

While some days may require courage to continue to hope, we can join Jeremiah in trusting that God will come through for us.

Let's see what good future God has in store for us and how the promised Messiah—known to us as Jesus—is the best part of God's plan for us.

DAY 26

An Audience of One

Fear of the LORD is the foundation of true knowledge,

but fools despise wisdom and discipline.

Proverbs 1:7

No matter our age or background, we can all find ourselves following the path of fearing people more than God. Worrying about the opinions of others will always get us into big trouble. Living to please the spectators on the road of faith leads to manipulation, worry, and disappointment—and ultimately to discipline from a loving God who wants to lead us back to Him as our source of hope. To find the source of true and lasting hope, we must worry less about what others think and more about obeying God.

We need to evaluate what is bigger in our lives: people and circumstances, or God? When we live like Jeremiah—putting fear of God over fear of people or circumstances—the road is not problem-free, but it is blessed. When we live to please others, we might please some people but disappoint others in the process.

When those stones of disapproval come flying at you, as they inevitably will, remember there is One who is crazy about you. His name is Jesus, and He wants you to follow His path because He adores you and knows the dangers of chasing the approval of others. No matter your situation, look to an audience of One who longs to bless you as you dare to live His way.

While people may let us down, God's promises never fail. He promised to send us a Savior because sin separates us from Him. Jeremiah taught about this promised Messiah who would bring us true and lasting hope.

Prayer

Lord,

I admit that I sometimes listen to the opinions of others instead of Your voice. Forgive me for the times I've feared rejection, sought approval, or changed my course of action to please people rather than follow You. Give me eyes to see when I'm living to meet others' expectations instead of Your purposes for me. Remind me that Your approval is enough and that Your way leads to true peace and lasting hope. In Jesus's name I pray, amen.

What decision(s) are you facing? Who might you be trying to please in your choice?

What are some areas where you may be concerned with the opinions of others more than trusting or obeying God?

How can you recognize when you are choosing or chasing the approval of others instead of following God's path for you?

What might help you remember that the approval of others is impossible to achieve or maintain?

DAY 27

Good Plans
Ahead

This is what the LORD says: "You will be in Babylon for seventy years. But then I will come and do for you all the good things I have promised, and I will bring you home again."

Jeremiah 29:10

No matter how bleak things may seem, God can work even the worst of circumstances together for our good. Jeremiah 29:11 says that God has good plans for His people. However, in Jeremiah 29:10, we find that His people will be in exile for seventy years.

Jeremiah 29:11 is not a promise to make life problem-free. It is an assurance to love and bless us even when times are tough.

God wants to bless us—to give us rest, hope, and peace. And these are good plans! However, because God knows that we cannot have these things apart from Him and that we are prone to wander, sometimes He allows difficult circumstances so that we will come back to Him. God knows and understands our bent toward sin. That's why He sent Jesus as a sacrifice, prophesying about Him through Jeremiah so many years before His coming. Ultimately, God's best plan for all who follow Him is spending eternity with Him. Though in this life there is much suffering, in the next there will be no tears. Even if the world crumbles around us or we must face many years in a difficult circumstance, we can know with confidence that God's plans are good because one day we will see Him face-to-face. Talk about a future and a hope!

Prayer

For today's prayer time, write down a difficult or painful situation in your life. Pause and ask God what good He is gleaning in the midst of it. Write down what you hear Him saying to you.

In what ways have you experienced God working through difficult circumstances to draw you closer to Him?

How can you find peace in knowing that God's good plans sometimes involve seasons of difficulty or waiting?

How does understanding that God's plans are ultimately for your good change the way you view challenges in your life?

How does the hope of eternity with Jesus spark your hope in your day-to-day life?

DAY 28

Hope That Brings Us Back

"I have loved you, my people, with an everlasting love.

With unfailing love I have drawn you to myself."

Jeremiah 31:3

Even in the midst of the promised punishment for sin, we see God's longing for His people (Jeremiah 31:3).

God offers hope for people who are willing to follow Him, to those who are willing to return to Him and seek His will for them. Followers of Jesus may endure a lot of difficulty; they may face times of uncertainty or times of loneliness, but they have learned that one day in close connection with Him is better than a thousand days elsewhere (Psalm 84:10). God offers hope to those who have learned to trust in Him through their struggles.

Even Jeremiah grew weary of suffering at times and got very discouraged. God continually encouraged him and called him to persevere in faith even when he didn't understand why no one seemed to be responding to his messages:

This is how the LORD responds:

"If you return to me, I will restore you
    so you can continue to serve me.
If you speak good words rather than worthless ones,
    you will be my spokesman.
You must influence them;
    do not let them influence you!"

Jeremiah 15:19

No matter if your world seems unstable in every direction, God offers you hope even through your pain. Like Jeremiah, some of our greatest times of intimacy with God come in moments of desperation when we realize how dependent on Him we truly are.

Prayer

For today's prayer time, write out a letter to God describing any weariness you feel in your life. Then listen for what He wants to say to you in response.

Dear God,

Amen.

How have you seen God continually draw you to Himself?

How does your understanding of God's love impact the way you view difficult circumstances in your life?

How can you cultivate that deep connection with God, especially during challenging times?

Jeremiah faced great discouragement, but God encouraged him to persevere. Think of areas in your life where you feel weary or disheartened. What might it look like to keep trusting, serving, and obeying God in this season?

DAY 29

The Promised Messiah

"For the time is coming,"
    says the LORD,
"when I will raise up a righteous descendant
    from King David's line.
He will be a King who rules with wisdom.
    He will do what is just and right throughout the land.
And this will be his name:
    'The LORD Is Our Righteousness.'
In that day Judah will be saved,
and Israel will live in safety."

Jeremiah 23:5-6

We find the hope of the promised Messiah throughout Jeremiah's writings. Jeremiah didn't know His name but referred to Him as the LORD Is Our Righteousness, who would save the people from sin.

God gave Jeremiah glimpses of a new covenant of grace and hope through this promised Messiah. While Jeremiah didn't know every detail about the cross or the Resurrection, he still placed his hope in this future Messiah. The sacrifices, the temple, the priesthood, and many of the other religious practices of Jeremiah's day all pointed to Jesus.

We have the privilege of reading Jeremiah's prophecies from this side of the cross. We see the fulfillment of his words through the lens of the person and work of Christ. We find the source of our hope in Jesus, the One who paid the price for your sin and mine. Our hope is built on Him alone. His death and resurrection give us a reason to hope in this life and the next. When we choose to fix our minds on Jesus (Hebrews 12:2), it gives us perspective for everything else we go through.

Prayer

For today's prayer, compose a psalm of thanks to Jesus for the peace and hope you have because of Him.

Why is it important that Jesus Is our righteousness? (hint: read 2 Corinthians 5:21)

How does knowing that Jesus fulfilled prophecies—written hundreds of years before His birth—give you hope in your day-to-day life?

How can Jesus's death and resurrection provide perspective to your life right now?

What are some practical ways you can keep your focus on Christ, especially in moments of difficulty or uncertainty?

DAY 30

Full Access

Yet I still dare to hope
    when I remember this:

The faithful love of the LORD never ends!
    His mercies never cease.
Great is his faithfulness;
    his mercies begin afresh each morning.

Lamentations 3:21-23

What does knowing Jesus mean to you? Think about this: if you could have access to a great Christian leader in our day, who would it be? Now imagine if that person gave you his or her personal phone number and said, "Call or text me anytime you have questions or are struggling. I will pray for you, counsel you, and encourage you." Would you lose the number and never contact the person? Or would you call often to build a relationship?

The question facing us is this: are we taking full advantage of our full access to the One who is our source of hope? Others can help us, but that doesn't compare to what God offers us through a relationship with Him. Although sin separated us from God, Christ restores our relationship through His sacrifice on the cross. So now we can enjoy friendship with a holy God. How can you take more advantage of the full access you've been given through Christ?

Jeremiah poured out his heart to God. He asked questions, listened for answers, softened his heart, and dared to hope even when life circumstances seemed to go from bad to worse.

Jeremiah dared to hope even in an unstable world. His messages about surrender, idolatry, listening, heart issues, personal responsibility, and hope in the promised Messiah hit very close to home as we attempt to navigate the difficulties in our own lives. Even if your circumstances do not budge an inch or perhaps intensify, I pray that your hope grows because of God's steadfast love and rich, new mercies.

Although some days can feel like we are in the bottom of a pit with Jeremiah, I have found that my greatest struggles have become some of God's greatest triumphs in my life. He has used these difficulties to draw me nearer to Him. I pray that this is true for you as well and that we can continue to dare to hope together through whatever tomorrow may bring.

Prayer

Thank You, God, for the incredible access I have to You through Jesus. I can call on You anytime, and You are always ready to listen, guide, and love me. Forgive me for not fully embracing this gift of relationship with You, for taking it for granted or turning to others when the answer is already, always in You.

Thank You for Your steadfast love, which never ends, and for the new mercies You give me each morning. Even when life feels overwhelming, I dare to hope because I know You are with me, working in my heart and bringing me closer to You. May I grow in trust and hope as I lean into Your faithfulness, no matter my circumstances.

Continually draw me nearer, Lord, and may I always remember that my greatest hope is always found in You.

In Jesus's name, amen.

Today, harvest the fruits of your journey of hope over the last thirty days with God. Look back through the previous pages and recall below the important truths God has spoken to you.

Now think about the ways God has answered your prayers, offered His presence, and given you hope! Write about those ways below.

Notes

Notes